Allegro

John Claiborne Isbell

Allegro

John Claiborne Isbell

Omni-Media Publishing
Edinburg, TX

Copyright © 2018 by John Claiborne Isbell.

All rights reserved.

ISBN 978-1-7328280-1-8

Acknowledgements:

Some of these poems first appeared on the Eratosphere website: "Preamble," "Clerihews," "Good Dog," and "Lemonade." Just about all of them were emailed to a dedicated group of readers in England and America: Bill, Maggie, Andy, Todd and Judy, Hermine, Amber, Alexander, Zélie, and Susan. They've been patiently receiving poetry emails from me for some years, and this is my chance to say, *Thank you all.*

I'd also like to thank my splendid editor, Anne Estevis, who helped to launch this project and also introduced me to my gifted art director, Suanne Goings, and my fine publisher, Steven Ramirez, who all helped to make this dream a reality.

Omni-Media Publishing
Edinburg, TX

Dedication

To Margarita goes this book.
To see my love, you can just look.

Other Books by this Author

The Birth of European Romanticism: Truth and Propaganda in Staël's De L'Allemagne, Cambridge: Cambridge University Press (1994).

The People's Voice: A Romantic Civilization, 1776-1848, Lilly Library, Bloomington, IN (1996).

Madame de Staël: Oeuvres de jeunesse, Paris: Desjonquères (1997).

Table of Contents

11   Foreword

13   Preamble

14   Sweat and Spit

15   Clerihews

19   The Muse That Screwed Me

20   Web

21   Functional Sonnet

22   Starbucks I Have Known

23   Morning Duties

24   Serenade

25   The Cigarette

26   Level Best

27   Pig Sonnet

28   The Best Revenge

29	The Prevention of Art
30	Migration
31	Stellar Destiny
32	Tit-for-Tat
33	Morning Poem
34	Work to Do
35	Hamster and Wheel
36	Invitation
37	Lament
38	Secret Santa
39	A Summer That Has Gone
40	Good Dog
41	Phobia
42	A Song Designed to Please
43	Glass

44	Ornamental Pond
45	The Seven Plots They Say Exist
47	What Bores Me
48	Where I Begin
49	The Parrot and the Crow
50	Lemonade
51	World Cup Semifinal Kit
52	The Wide-Mouthed Frog Joke
53	Lilliput
54	Itineraries
55	The Mighty Clouds of Joy
56	The Things We Think Are True
57	Because
59	Sin
60	Ultimate

61   Far Shore

62   Obscurity in Poetry

63   Envoi

64   About the Author

Foreword

To me, John Claiborne Isbell is somewhat of an enigma: a native-born American who speaks with a distinctive British accent, a mild-mannered university teacher who plays on an Ultimate Frisbee team, and a poet who can pen a whimsical clerihew minutes after finishing an intricate Petrarchan sonnet.

When first I met John and his poetry, it seemed to me he wrote exclusively non-rhyming poems – "free verse," as I call them. I said nothing about this for some time, and then one day recently, after editing a large number of his poems, I casually asked John, "Don't you ever write poems that rhyme?" My question soon started a barrage of dings emanating from my cell phone indicating I was receiving emails. This activity began one Saturday night and continued off and on until the next morning. The emails were poems from John – of course – all rhyming.

"Do you have enough of these poems for a chapbook?" was my next question for John. He certainly did when he added these new poems to some he had written over the previous years. This book is the pleasant outcome. So, if you enjoy Shakespearean or Petrarchan sonnets, clerihews, or poetry in general, you should delight in the poems of John Claiborne Isbell.

Marjorie Anne Estevis, Ed.D
Edinburg, Texas

Preamble

I'm leafing through my MSS.;
I've twelve of them, and I confess
that reading through them is a chore.
I've other things to read, and more

to do before the sun comes up.
There's only so much that a cup
of coffee makes appealing. But
I've almost finished, and can cut

this out in a bare hour or so.
How much I've read them, I don't know;
perfection is a losing game;
you never win, and there's no blame

in that; we try, but it won't work.
We will be brought up with a jerk
by death's dark door. Progressively,
our lives, our art will cease to be.

Shan't we be perfect after death?
What I say is: *Don't hold your breath.*

Sweat and Spit

Mine is a muse that treads the ground.
She does not soar; she does not fly
on saffron wing through evening sky
to me. She is not hanging round

when I get home from work, or found
where rainbows end, or passing by
when I'm stopped at a light. I try
to pen a line that will astound,

and she erases it. Instead
she makes me earn my daily bread
the hard way, out of sweat and spit.

Her spectacles make her look smart.
She shows up when it suits her; art
is like that, there's no taming it.

Clerihews

The elephant or pachyderm
will never trouble to confirm
if he remembers all they claim
or else forgets things just the same.

The three-toed sloth
doth
move with some deliberation.
This is also true of people in high station.

Cuttlefish
is a dish
some will consume with gusto.
I will only eat it just so.

Upon one leg, the heron
is staring
into the pond for fish.
They are its dearest wish.

The flamingo
of Santo Domingo
is not a *rara avis*.
Such is the world God gave us.

A male red-breasted nuthatch
simply can't match
the bird of paradise for feathers.
But you will find him in all weathers.

A reminder:
the sidewinder
is a highly poisonous snake.
Therefore to pet it would be a mistake.

One of the things about a cat
is that
he won't come when you're calling.
There are some who find this appalling.

The orangutan,
or Man
of the Forest, in Malay,
from the woods will rarely stray.

The chimpanzee,
unlike you and me,
is not an urban dweller.
He is a woodland feller.

The mountain gorilla
might enjoy a glass of sarsaparilla,
since he is a vegetarian.
Though the silverback is a bit of a disciplinarian.

The buffalo or bison
appears on the horizon
in numbers less immense
than in the days people lived out there in tents.

The Creature from the Black Lagoon
would swoon
if Julie Adams loved it back.
But she does not, alack!

Speaking of mythical creatures
whose actual features
are familiar to no man,
how about the sasquatch or abominable snowman?

There is no defeat'll
persuade a dung beetle
that dung's not for rolling.
I however would rather go bowling.

Diplodocus
would swear and cuss
if you called him a Tyrannosaurus;
otherwise, he tends to bore us.

The tufted titmouse
will not grouse
or complain about cold weather,
being all afeather.*

*NB: This last word is not in the dictionary.
I sometimes say the same of *gullible*, to surprise the unwary.

The Muse That Screwed Me

The night she came in through my open casement,
she promised that our time in bed would hurt.
Still, eiderdown is better than the basement,
and all my pain worked to keep me alert.

Not many poets write of quiet comfort
in love; it's joy or pain all down the line.
Love's one thing, but the way to art's discomfort,
as vintners crush the grape upon the vine.

My Muse screwed me twelve years ago but good.
She may return, though we've both understood
my heart's finesse at loving overseas;

thus, vintners, who grow weary of their fruit
and wish for apples, yet are resolute,
as I don't leave my Muse for other shes.

Web

From my fat abdomen, I spin
line after line of verse. Within

its tight web, the unwary may
little by little lose their way

and come to grief. You can't expect
each step you take to be direct

as you proceed along this path.
What's left is just the aftermath –

another victim in my game.
There's really nobody to blame

except myself. I hold each thread
in this hand. Try TV instead.

Functional Sonnet

It was a bid to dance for 14 verses.
Hendecasyllables he had always loved,
based on his theory Dante could be improved.
It was a flash of passes and traverses.

The losers would be ferried off in hearses;
the winner would take home the prize, if only
he or she knew, while standing on the lonely
peak of art, what were gifts and what were curses.

A pass, a thrust, and blood flared on a necklace.
The rule of art is brief: winner takes all.
A hand went cold; a heart once bold and reckless

stopped in the beat of an impartial second.
As partners fell, the winner at this ball
danced faster – working less than all had reckoned.

Starbucks I Have Known

The most beautiful thing in Tokyo is McDonald's . . .
–Andy Warhol

I speak to the *barista* in
Bulgarian, though T shirts here
are all in English. I begin
to give my order, disappear.

At Charles de Gaulle, the coffee's dear;
and yet, it seems I cannot win
attention from the staff. I fear
that I'll grow angry as I spin

my wheels; I almost make my own.
I'm talking on the telephone
in Punxsutawney, in L.A.,

as the line clears and I am served
my Grande Latte. I've observed
my taste in Starbucks is *au fait*.

Morning Duties

What needed doing has been done.
The pot is off the hob. The bread
is sliced. The bed is freshly made;
the floor is swept. The day's begun.

Each day has duties. There are none
more pressing than the marmalade
the bread requires. Who is in bed,
when in the East, we see the sun

break the horizon? This is how
the morning speaks. There may be more
that noon and evening have in store,

but I am quite content for now.
Do what needs doing when it's due;
these words are my advice to you.

Serenade

The noise of evening falls away.
The books are closed; the teeth are brushed.
Outside, the very stars are hushed.
The toys and dolls in their array

await the morning. As the day
takes leave of us, there's nothing rushed
in its farewell. The toilet's flushed,
the kids are in bed, where they'll stay

until the sun comes up again.
Like a cool breeze across the plain
that moves the wheat and lifts the quail,

peace settles on the parents' hearts.
And soon the task of sleeping starts:
the bout with dream. It will prevail.

The Cigarette

I bummed a cigarette off of a friend;
the cylinder was white, but brown inside,
the crushed leaves packed in paper to the end,
just as an animal will have its hide.

A ciggy tells you you have time to spend;
its slow burn fills your chest like mortal pride,
carcinogens and nicotine that blend
with tar to coat your lungs from the inside.

A cigarette's best smoked without a filter:
to keep one says the choice is out of kilter,
a nod to fear dressed up in caution's name.

Your cigarette says life is but a game –
a pleasant row along the banks of death,
which comes to all. Take pleasure in your breath.

Level Best

Have I outplayed my demons? Can a man
achieve as much? The demons hold the cards.
I have constructed something from the shards
that I was left with, and it is my plan

to live my life content. For in the span
of days that Fate has granted to the bards,
we have a choice. Hoist with their own petards
are those who choose to sorrow. I'm no fan

of demons, but my own I have embraced;
thus I remove their power. I have chased
the bird of happiness home to its nest,

and here I perch. We are not made for trees,
you may remark, but we do as we please
in this life. And I do my level best.

Pig Sonnet

The die is cast – a throw into the night –
a roll of sixes as the bouncing stops.
Each verse of this art is a thing of light,
a gamble big enough to bring the cops.

A sonnet's stanzas are a welcome sight,
as, in the Autumn, are the bursting crops.
Their green and gold stand tall against the blight,
too proud to feed the pigs amid the slops.

The velvet of the table lures the eye;
I throw again; the croupier halts a bet;
the dice bound, turn, resign, and then they die,

like thirsty fields of corn when there's no wet.
I'd never known an ear could be so dry.
The pigs are hungry though, so don't you fret.

The Best Revenge

If you can sing, then sing right now,
to greet the sun like any bird.
The wise propose that life's absurd,
that all we do will take a bow

and leave the stage without a word
when our time's up. I won't allow
defeat; in fact, I don't care how
you feel; I don't care what you've heard;

the best revenge is living well.
Pick up your heart. I cannot tell
what shape it's in if you sing out

as birds do when the day begins.
It's time to reckon up your wins;
so let's do that. And don't you pout.

The Prevention of Art

When marbled contours brook no human touch –
his hands at fault, that do not know to *feel* –
then is your form more perfect and more real,
to belly life, and name all else too much.

Nor can art make me love the vaulted face
a hollow sky will turn on all our deeds,
as I do love the face of each who reads:
though her each eye wink out, in death's embrace.

So, if infinity is but a crutch
your sculptor grapples when he tires of life –
I'll drop my artist's gloves with you, my wife,
and laugh, to feel you *move* beneath my touch!

This bed, whose confines seal our common trust,
will bed our heirs when marble turns to dust.

Migration

The Valley gets a little rain,
to wet the palm trees and the *taquerías*.
The winter flocks are here again,
the Winter Texans. They are glad to see us.

Stellar Destiny

Tonight, the stars are out in force,
unnumbered as the ocean strand,
as forest leaves. And in their course
across the heavens, they command

attention and perhaps assent
from all of us who are awake
to see them. The improvident
may wonder if it's their mistake

or the stars' work that's left them skint.
It's in the stars, folks like to say,
as if there were a starry tint
to life on Earth. And as we stray

from virtue or from grace, we lift
our gaze into the nighttime sky
in search of meaning. We may shift
the blame, but we should not rely

on answers or apologies
for our mistakes from up above.
High overhead, stars take their ease;
and our fate fits us like a glove.

Tit-for-Tat

I'm at my desk at 5 a.m.,
and working on a requiem
for all that ever walked on Earth.
It's true, death does come after birth –
that's just the way that we are made,
like cars or lightbulbs. The parade
of all that's lived continues on,
it won't be stopped. And as the dawn
breaks on the Gulf and heads my way,
I find I have not much to say
about what we already know.
On Earth, the living come and go
like renters in a property.
The landlord is an absentee,
he'll barely fix the pipes. We park
in the front yard, and after dark,
disturb the neighbors. Is it fair
to think the landlord should be there
to do more than collect his check?
He weights the dice; he stacks the deck,
I hear you say. And that may be.
But it is pure insanity
to hope for better in this place:
to hope for joy, to hope for grace
is a fool's errand. All that lives
will perish. If the future gives
some new hope, I can't speak to that.
Thus life plays out. It's tit-for-tat.

Morning Poem

It's almost seven, and the light of dawn
begins to fill the eastern sky. My wife
is at her desk; this is a quiet life
for both of us. The grackles on the lawn

and in the trees are silent, though the hum
of city traffic reaches us. I sit
in my kimono on the bed, and it
is covered by a quilt. Were you to come

through our front door, you'd see we've breakfasted:
the day's begun, though we're not dressed. Today
we'll meet with our department chair, to say
our thanks, and ask some questions. If instead

you stood outside and gazed at the grey sky
of early morning, you might see the birds
that head toward the sunrise. All the words
I'm writing won't describe them passing by.

Work to Do

The sun is lifting in the East
to start the day. And so, released
from their long journey through the night,
the planets leave the scene. It's quite
majestic. I've seen fifty years
and more of daybreaks, and the gears
of Heaven speak like my own hand.
The night's unable to withstand
the press of day; and all that dreams
succumbs to waking. Daylight seems
to hold the field; and work is done,
decisions made, as everyone
takes day for granted. Yet again
night will loom up across the plain;
tools will be downed, and eyes will shut.
The planets in their well-worn rut
will journey back across the sky;
the stars will shine; and you and I
will sleep, will dream. Then dawn anew
will break, and bring us work to do.

Hamster and Wheel

Around once more, the spinning wheel
conveys the hamster. What we feel
as we behold its fruitless quest
will vary. Saying *I am blessed*
when asked how she was doing, one
homeless shelter client spun
my head around. I learned from that
to slow in judgement. What a rat
feels in the maze escapes our ken;
nor is that really news. *Amen*,
we say in church, as if the time
to see a change is *never*. I'm
not in that camp, for anything
should have its end. A piece of string
is just as long as it should be,
thank goodness. No epiphany
will sway my mind. The hamster's run
will free him; the task he's begun
will end, and he can come to rest.
The homeless lady, unimpressed
by the mundane, anticipates
a new dawn daily, and equates
her morning with one blessed by God.
Let our wheel turn; beneath the sod
we'll have a chance to rest our feet.
Now – like that string – this song's complete.

Invitation

The choir of angels at my door
are shedding light on my front lawn.
And if they've come to greet the dawn –
as angels do – then nothing more

precisely suited to my mind
could be imagined. I'm a man
who does the same; and when I can,
I'll peer out through the shuttered blind

to see the angels lift in song.
The sun is up, and so are we;
I make the point excitedly,
so all who wake can sing along.

Lament

Some things are best forgotten. In
the scheme of things, you can't expect
your math to always be correct,
your free concerto to begin.

About the time I went to school,
I learned these truths, though it oppressed
the mind to be just second-best –
to swipe the milk, to flout the rule.

I'm older now, and all I've learned
slips from my mind as water might.
A blessing. Let's not be uptight,
or mourn the stupor we have earned.

Secret Santa

The gift I gave the angels was
a thing they do not have, because
all gifts are better so. You don't
take coals to Newcastle; it won't
surprise the mind, delight the eye.
You want a person passing by
to say: *That must have made them glad.*
To find a thing they'd never had:
that was my task. And so, in rhyme,
I gave ten minutes of my time
into their holy keeping. They
accepted it with grace. A stray
dog barked. A truck backed up. I made
a cup of coffee. And displayed
across the heavens were the stars.
The angels, taking their guitars,
set this to music. For a song
pleases the Lord. There's nothing wrong
with joining in the angels' choir,
at 4 a.m. or so. Entire
religions have been built on less.
So is this true? You can but guess.

A Summer That Has Gone

The wine I pour into the cup
delights me. As I fill it up,
I feel wine wash across my brain
prospectively, and drink again.

Wine is a toxin, and my cells
do battle with it, which compels
my mind to ecstasy. It's not
a new discovery; the rot

of the must in the barrel leads
to this dark liquor, and the seeds
of trance are born. What I desire
is something to which men aspire

around this blue globe. How should one
describe the taste of wine? The sun
and rain of summer, and the ground
beneath the grape are gathered round

in juice that fills the bottle, and
a man may taste them. In my hand
I hold a summer that has gone.
Time passes, but the wine lives on.

Good Dog

Every day, I come to where
my owner should get off the train
to greet me. I am there again
today. My owner is not there,

and I am older than I was
in days when he would walk me home.
The days tick like a metronome
into the past. And just because

I'm at my spot, I think he should
come smiling in, give me a pat,
say, *Good dog*. This is where I'm at
when he is due. This dog is good.

Phobia

I'm not afraid of nothing, I would peep
in my brief youth. Yet, in the tourist town
of Brighton once, I swam out past the pier
and felt a panic seize me. I saw clear
through that grey roiling water, further down
than where the sharks swam, to the alien deep.

A Song Designed to Please

This is a song designed to please.
I wrote it in the dead of night.
I did not write it on my knees,
but fashioned it for your delight

while sitting in my dungarees;
they're in blue denim, splashed with white.
I'd sing about the birds and bees,
but have no time, for I am quite

determined to be short and sweet.
And that's a wrap, my song's complete.

Glass

The room reflected in the glass
will calmly let its contents pass
from sight, or reappear, as we
adjust the glass, or let it be.

Just now, it holds my visage. This
is no surprise; the edifice
has seen me nightly, and my face
can come and go without a trace

on this bright surface. That is how
things work: my mirror will allow
the greatest sinners to reflect
their image, it's not circumspect.

Ornamental Pond

A red bridge through the leaves, and on its arch,
a father and his daughter. They admire
the ornamental pond below. The march
of time does not affect them. I conspire

with nature to review them. Where I sit
are fallen leaves, as if in fact the past
still shaped the future here. The swallows flit
through blue air, and the sun is moving fast

as it knows how toward its western end.
There's lichen in the rocks. The lawn is rich
with yellow flowers. People don't attend
to my work. It goes off without a hitch.

The Seven Plots They Say Exist

I'm fond of fairy tales, because
they recognize that there are laws
to telling stories, or what I
call *fiction*. That it is a lie

is number one. If you must state
that your work is the truth, relate
how you acquired the text you print,
journal or correspondence. Hint

at how it was produced; we will
need proof your fiction fits the bill
of something written out of need.
Once that is done, you may proceed

to fabricate. Do not begin:
On Tuesday, I was drinking gin,
when you were not. There's little art
to making truth up from the start,

as modern novels often do.
I recommend that you review
the place of stories in the mind,
as children see it. You may find

the seven plots they say exist
repeating on your page. Persist
in fiction, but don't be afraid
to mark the fiction you have made

as fairy tales will, where the plot
is freed from truth, and we are not
surprised at magic. Stories speak
to us as dreams do, in oblique

and broken fashion. They may be
a lie, and yet can help us see
a truth we'd missed before we heard
their dancing phrase, their pregnant word.

What Bores Me

You'd think that it might vex me more
to sit behind and not before;
to always live on borrowed terms.
What can I say? That eating worms

can be done in the nicest seat?
*A busy day is not complete
without a worm or two*, the man
opines, and eats one. People can

be sad or happy anywhere,
that's hardly news. I don't compare
the hand that I've been dealt with yours,
I draw another card. It bores

me to do otherwise; the game
has highs and lows, and there's no blame
to playing well with what you hold.
Fortune, they say, *favors the bold*,

so make your choices and believe
in them; that's how it works. Receive
the fallout with an open heart;
you've played the game, and that's a start.

Where I Begin

There's very little I can do
to be myself instead of you.
This is no game. When you catch cold,
I catch it too. When you grow old,

I age. And when you find a thing
of interest, that's when I fling
my own tastes to the wind, and share
in what you feel. *There is no there*

there, Gertrude Stein wrote, and for me
those words ring true. I cannot see
where you end and where I begin.
If you have lost, I do not win,

and when you win, I celebrate.
Those who are married can relate,
I think, to what I'm saying here:
it isn't that I hold you dear,

it's that I do not draw a line
between our lives, and you decline
to do so likewise. In the end,
this is a state I recommend.

The Parrot and the Crow

Two birds known for their voices met one day
through a thin pane of glass.
"Caw!", said the crow, in language not our own,
"I stand on branches or the fresh-mown grass
to sing, while you spend your days in a cage."
"Polly want a cracker," said the parrot.
The crow continued: "I hear what you say,
but with the glass there's nothing I can do.
We neither of us sing like other birds:
my only word is 'Caw,' while you've outgrown
the tongues of birds for men's. I'd like to know
what you've found out about this glittering world."
"Who's a pretty boy, then?" said the parrot.
"I may not have your crest, but there's no need
to mock me," said the crow, "I came in friendship.
But after the abuse you've hurled,
I will be on my way."
The moral of this story's clear indeed:
a thinker may be in a mute embedded,
while fancy talkers may be empty-headed.

Lemonade

Myfanwy hovers at the door.
A rainy day. And who'll come out
to throw a ball, to run and shout,
to sit at tea? A nagging doubt
consumes her. In her narrow store

of birthdays, there's no precedent
for weather. It is almost time
to hear the happy doorbell chime.
She turns, as if in pantomime,
to scowl at Edward, who was sent

to let her know the table's laid;
which, more or less, he does. The cake
has seven candles. It may take
a sort of miracle to make
Myfanwy's heart the lemonade

of troubles overcome. Around
this time, the doorbell rings, and she
stands at the door. Who can it be?
She turns the waiting knob to see:
it's Annie, wet, but safe and sound.

World Cup Semifinal Kit

When England kicked the ball to score,
England supporters wanted more.
It's a game of two halves, they said.
The players muttered, *On me 'ead*,
and that is where they beat the Swedes.
But it may be the contest needs
no space beyond the bottom line:
2-0. The net is made of twine
and England put the ball in it.
Now World Cup Semifinal kit
will grace the shops. How time has flown
since that day Germany was shown
the door in 1966!
I'm happy as a pile of bricks.

The Wide-Mouthed Frog Joke

The Wide-Mouthed Frog Joke, that requires
two hands, and someone who aspires
to humor more than dignity,
can please a child of only three
or someone with kids of that age.
I would relate it on the page,
but sadly, it would miss its mark.
Today, while sitting in the park,
I told it to Allan, who's now
eleven; and he knit his brow
to fathom what was going on
until the punchline – then the dawn
broke on his face, he laughed for joy.
That's why I tell it to each boy
or girl entrusted to my care,
as uncles will. While sitting there,
one might as well make children laugh.
Those lines could be my epitaph.

Lilliput

Among the Lilliputians, Gulliver
discovered he was bound, as if the air
had fashioned thread to hold him. This was not
so very new a thing. The little plot

in gossamer, yet they will weave their spell
on those born bigger. There's no way to tell
a spark the outside air's no friend; a flame
must be encouraged. *No one is to blame*

when bright lights fail, you might opine. And I
point out the planets in the night-time sky,
whose light comes from the sun. For what is bright
sheds light on what's around it. My delight

in greatness stems from this. In Lilliput,
where things are small, there is a well-worn rut
men come to know – a warm bath of the soul.
All very well, when warm baths are your goal.

Itineraries

Up and down, up and down
run the people in this town.

Round about, round about,
spins the planet. If you're out

at sunset you will see that done:
the day's gone by; the night's begun.

To and fro, to and fro;
that is our business here below.

Back and forth, back and forth
goes everything you meet on Earth.

The Mighty Clouds of Joy

What gospel preaches at its best
is that life's hard. I've second-guessed
myself enough that I respect
those who choose not to. I'll project
a world of thinking onto art
if need be, I am very smart;
but I like simple things. *I don't
feel no ways tired*, a song I won't
attempt to sing spells out. You can
find here the measure of a man:
tall as the sky or short as sin.
This is a place we might begin.

The Things We Think Are True

The holy burns through what is everyday
as flame will burn through paper. If your eyes
can open, let them open. As we play
at good and bad, at big and small, the prize

escapes our fingers. All the work we've done
amounts to nothing, we might just as well
have placed our hope in candy, or begun
to hop and waddle to escape from Hell.

We are so frail! And yet, with every word
we speak, with every step we take, a light
transfigures us. Our lives may be absurd
seen from below, but as a bird in flight

is not a bird aground, so we release
into the absolute. We may be blind,
we may be deaf. But daylight does not cease
when we sleep in. That's when our dreaming mind

puts day into our dreaming, and we wake.
All this to say: the things we think are true
or urgent are not always so. I take
a sort of comfort in that *aperçu*.

Because

My inner two-year-old is sure
that all is kosher to the pure,
that wide-eyed is the way to be.
I do not doubt his honesty;

and yet, I feel that there is scope
in life to be adult. I cope
with tears and tantrums as I can,
with all the moods that keep a man

from paying taxes, raising kids.
I think that since first hominids
stood up or used a tool, we've seen
resistance to the Holocene

from those who built it. Let your mind
stay innocent, and you will find
that some things simply don't get done.
But does what's lost match what is won

when we act as if we were two?
Does being old match being new?
Perhaps it does. Yet it may seem
ungracious to renounce the dream,

to say goodbye to Neverland.
It's true that life is stale and bland
without the fire that youth provides.
Let others toil. If I take sides,

I'll choose the child that I once was.
You may ask why. I'll say, *Because*.

Sin

What did the preacher speak about?
He spoke about sin.
And what did he say?
He said he was against it.
—Calvin Coolidge

About the time that I begin
to contemplate a life of sin,
I find that I am just too tired
to leave my desk. I am inspired
by the great sinners of the past,
who nailed their colors to the mast
in all they did, in all they wrote.
They are the sort of folks I quote;
yet I am bookish and demure.
Thus by default my life is pure,
I really don't get up to much –
and like a rabbit's in his hutch,
my days are circumscribed and tame.
Of course, I've just myself to blame
my great revolt has not occurred.
And that will be my final word.

Ultimate

Up and down the field we ran,
throwing things and catching things.
We moved in unison; a man
will do this. All our offerings

we gave to air that they be caught.
We leapt, we dived. We stuck a hand
out into air, and thus we brought
our team downfield. The things we planned,

we moved to execute, until
the team we faced got in the way.
We bent the world to match our will,
 and won our game. That's why we play.

Far Shore

The heads you'll see upon my shelves
were brought here from the Philippines.
How do they fare? *Things in themselves*,
says Kant, *escape us*. What this means

is that all we can do is look
and take a guess. So is there more
than wood to their carved eyes? A book
might tease this out. On their far shore,

where my aunt walked, a tree once grew;
a sculptor thought and carved a face.
How that tree looked, what that man knew,
has vanished into time and space

where there is no retrieving it.
And yet, the heads are here: a man,
a woman, by my Roman lit. –
Macrobius. I have no plan

to journey to the Philippines
to find what now does not exist.
On TV and in magazines
I've seen the place dissolve in mist.

Obscurity in Poetry

I might twine language into cord. I might
bend nature to my will, the way a boy
will bend a straw, the way a satellite
bends gravity around it. I'll annoy

those with a taste for clarity, despite
my page's glamor, and the *hoi polloi*
will not be reading. You will say I'm bright,
you'll look for hidden depth, and there is joy

in such a search, if that's your constitution.
If two plus two is four, I'll spell it out
in poetry. You may be left in doubt

as to your sums, but you'll be entertained
along the way, for I won't be constrained
by truth or syntax. That's my contribution.

Envoi

Go, little book; depart from me
into the world. Decidedly
we've laughed, we've shed a tear; we've seen
a thing or two. *A magazine*
does no less and is thrown away,
you tell me. *At the close of day,*
is that my fate – am I a brief
distraction? Is the tree in leaf
so soon to lose what made it green?
I say, *I'm not sure what you mean;*
for wit and grace will always find
a ready heart, a willing mind,
and those traits are your attributes
(we flatter when we're in cahoots).
So you move on. A bumblebee
will visit blooms successively;
the blooms will see bees come and go,
they're hardly loyal. Here below,
that's how life plays out. As we part,
I think of this, and steel my heart.

About the Author

John Claiborne Isbell, a descendant of Pocahontas and of the poet Thomas Wyatt, among others, was born in Seattle but grew up mostly in Western Europe: Italy, France, Germany, and the United Kingdom. He represented France in the European Ultimate Frisbee Championships, earned a Ph.D. in French at Cambridge University, and returned to America to teach at Indiana University.

There John published books on the European Romantics (notably Mme de Staël), along with the occasional poem. In 1996, his scholarship put him in *Who's Who in the World*.

Meanwhile, John continued to visit his aunt Frances in South Texas, as he had since childhood. He came south with his wife Margarita and son Aibek in 2015 to begin teaching French and German at the University of Texas – Rio Grande Valley. John also began writing poetry in earnest; some of his manuscripts recently placed as finalist or semifinalist for The Washington Prize (twice), The Brittingham & Felix Pollak Prizes, and The Gival Press Poetry Award. John's first published book of poems is light and it rhymes from start to finish; that as much as anything is why his wife suggested naming it *Allegro*.

www.ingramcontent.com/pod-product-compliance
Lightning Source LLC
Chambersburg PA
CBHW032215040426
42449CB00005B/613